Spencer Parker was caught in a never-ending shuffle between prisons and insane asylums. When his violent actions finally became uncontrollable, he asked God to remove the hostility and hatred. It was like a dream come true—until his sight was also taken from him. Find out how Spencer learned to accept and overcome his new handicap, using it for God's ministry. Now you can share the vision to which his blind eyes were opened.

BLIND SIGHT

Spencer Parker

Fleming H. Revell Company
Old Tappan, New Jersey

Scripture quotations not otherwise identified are based on the
King James Version of the Bible.

Scripture quotations identified RSV are from the Revised Standard Version of the Bible, copyrighted 1946, 1952, © 1971 and 1973.

LC# 77-18654

ISBN 0-8007-9006-5

Contents

TO the men and women in prison, with my prayer that they will be encouraged to seek the Lord who is their only hope

Acknowledgments

I am especially grateful to my many friends, whose lives, love, kindness, and encouragement over the years have made a very deep impact upon my life and challenged me to walk humbly before my Lord. Although I regret that I can mention only a few by name, this book would be incomplete without my saying how thankful I am for Mr. Ernest Chase and his late wife; Deputy Chief of Police John Dougherty and his wife; Matthew Rocco, my dear brother and partner in the Lord's work; Dalton Greene; and Pastor Grover Willcox and his wife.

I thank God for the Pocket Testament League, and for the blessing it is to work with this deeply devoted staff of Christians, who pray for me daily and have shared the pains and heartaches I experienced due to the loss of my vision. Detective Curtis Gilmore was used of the Lord to introduce me to the Pocket Testament League. J. Edward Smith stood by me, prayed for me, encouraged me, helped me, and permitted me to continue as a League missionary in spite of my handicap. I am also thankful for my dear wife and children—for their love, patience, and understanding. And how grateful I am for the abundant love, prayers, and support I've received from the Grace Reformed Church of Lansing, Illinois, and from Grace Church of Ridgewood, New Jersey.

It is impossible to measure the impact on my life of Mr. Jack Binns, who led me to the Lord twenty-two years ago, and the Reverend Stewart A. Snedeker, who patiently taught and instructed me from the Word of God.

I am also indebted to Adrianne Simmons and Larry Burke, who served as my eyes in proofreading the manuscript of this book.

There are many other friends who deserve special thanks, but whom I cannot acknowledge because of lack of space, but I do want to thank, as a group, my many brothers in Christ who are members of the Christian Lawmen's Fellowship of Northern New Jersey, which I serve as chaplain. I'm also grateful to the many who labor with me in distributing the Gospels of John.

Finally, my greatest appreciation and gratitude go to my Lord and Savior, Christ Jesus, who saved me and has entrusted me with His Word and the ministry of reconciliation.

1

". . . No Man Cared for My Soul"

As the cell door clanked shut behind me, I sighed slightly and waited for my breathing to adjust to the stale, sweat-soaked air in the prison. I had been in enough jails to know that I'd soon get used to it.

This time I was charged with breaking and entering. A few years before, it was armed robbery. Though I was barely twenty years old, cold concrete cubicles and steel bars had already taken the place of the warm home I had always sought, but could not find.

There was another inmate in the cell, and we were soon playing cards to while away the hours, gambling for our only possessions—a few cigarettes. As we got deeper into our card game, I found I was winning most of the other fellow's cigarettes—without cheating.

I had learned all about cheating in the bars and poolrooms I frequented on the outside. If someone caught me, I'd bully my way through by pulling out a gun or a knife. But it wasn't necessary to try any tricks with this inmate, because he wasn't much of a card player.

Unfortunately, he hated to lose as much as I loved to win. When I won all his cigarettes, he started yelling for the guards.

"He took my cigarettes!"

"I won them fair and square in a card game!" I protested to the burly guard who walked over, scowling, to our cell.

"Give the cigarettes back," the guard said.

"I'm not gonna give them back, because I won them!" I said defiantly.

Wearily, the guard gestured for one of his colleagues

to join him, and together they started dragging me out of my cell. One of them gave me a shove, followed it with a kick, and growled, "Wise guy!"

By this time, I was so upset that I struck back. Seeing a mop bucket just outside the cell, I lunged through the door, picked up the bucket, and hit one of my attackers in the stomach with the makeshift weapon. They quickly overpowered me and started pummelling me with their fists and feet. Half-dazed, I covered up as well as I could until they finally decided to stop. Then they roughly shoved me into the hallway and dragged me to a cell in solitary confinement.

I was furious. I started yelling at them, trying to tell them my side of the cigarette story, but they wouldn't listen. So I did a really stupid thing: I decided to *make* them listen. Pulling out some matches I still had in my pocket, I tore my mattress apart and set the whole thing on fire. *This way, they'll have to come down here and listen to what I have to say,* I thought.

The guards rushed downstairs, all right, but they didn't wait to listen to me. They put the fire out and didn't feed me that afternoon. A couple of hours later, two huge, muscular guys, carrying shackles and handcuffs, opened my cell door and said, "Okay, put your hands out in front of you."

When I refused, they quickly jumped me and wrestled me to the floor. Before I knew it, my arms and legs were in chains, and a straitjacket was strapped around my chest.

The head guard, who had been watching the action with some amusement, said, "All right, wise guy, the judge told us to send you to the crazy house."

I had been committed to the state prison for the criminally insane! When I walked through the doors of that institution, I immediately knew it was a place of the living dead. People were screaming, hollering, or just walking around in a stupor. They bathed me, shaved all my hair off, and gave me a hospital gown in place of my clothes.

Most of the time, I was kept in my cell. I even ate there. The only time I got out was to undergo special medical treatments, or for brief stays in a downstairs recreation room. But the recreation room didn't offer me much recreation or human companionship.

One of the inmates thought he was an airplane; another fancied he was a bird. I recall one man who had undergone a lobotomy—removal of part of the brain. He was completely out of touch with reality and spent most of his time walking around the room carrying several paper bags, always traveling to some place his troubled mind was leading him, but never quite reaching his destination.

I finally found three other men who were sane enough to join me in some card games. But after several sessions, the guards said they had heard we were conspiring to break out, so we lost our recreation privileges.

I spent all my time in my cell and was released only to get what the medical people called a "typhoid antibacteria shot." But the reactions I experienced didn't resemble those from any ordinary vaccination. There's no word in the dictionary to describe the effects of that drug—which I learned was probably part of chemical therapy to control my mind. I developed fever, nausea, cramps, and loss of hearing. I'd curl up in a knot on the floor of my cell, my body ice-cold.

Except for these treatments, the guards kept me in isolation for three months, without any clothing, or a mattress to sleep on. They kept the windows open and rarely flushed my toilet. Some nights, as I lay naked on the hard, cold concrete floor of my cell, with the overpowering stench from the toilet paralyzing my lungs and nostrils, I cried out, choking on my tears, "Why is this happening to me? Is it just because I got into a fight? *Why?*"

For the first time in my life, I began to seriously

think about the meaning of life and death. Desperately seeking mercy from somewhere, I racked my brain for anything I could remember about God or heaven or hell. Bits and pieces of information, things my mother had taught me, began to creep back into my consciousness. But I had never learned anything about how to find salvation, how to establish a relationship with God.

This inadequate search for divine help finally reached a dead end, and my thoughts turned with renewed power toward revenge. I had been abused and beaten down so much that I became a caged animal, living for only one purpose—to wreak destruction on my tormentors. I wanted to kill the two cops who had arrested and beaten me. I wanted to destroy a relative who had treated me poorly and had arranged for my first reformatory incarceration. I vowed I would kill them—and I always kept my word.

If only I had been told there was another way, a better way, I might have borne my suffering and gone on to have my life straightened out. But no one ever bothered to explain any other way to me. I had no way of knowing that a man by the name of David had cried out in similar anguish ages ago:

> I looked on my right hand, and beheld, but there was no man that would know me: refuge failed me; no man cared for my soul.
>
> Psalms 142:4

The difference between us was that David knew Someone was listening. I didn't.

2

Rootless

I was born into confusion. My last name was Tate, and somehow it became Parker, even though my mother's name was Currie Cunningham. I have no birth certificate, so I don't know when or where I was born. Some say my birthplace was Columbus, Mississippi, where I lived as a youngster; others say it was Macon, Georgia; and still others claim it was some port in the West Indies.

I know my mother was West Indian, and my earliest memory is of a nice, sunny day when we traveled a long time by boat. I'm inclined to think I'm West Indian, but I guess I'll never know for sure. I only saw my father once in my life, when I was about five or six. I recall him as a big, strapping man, but that was the first and last time I saw him. He walked out on us.

Even though confusion about my family roots surrounded me as a youngster, I was enveloped by maternal love. I came down with hepatitis when I was very little, and Mom spent most of her time caring for me. She and I became the closest of pals, and she never referred to me as Spencer, but always called me "Son," or "my son." When I was feeling bad, she'd take me in her arms and carry me out to a vegetable patch we had behind our home in Mississippi.

"Now, let me tell you about those peanuts and to-matoes," she'd say, and I'd soon forget how sick I was.

Even though we had to walk a great distance, my mother always took me to church with her. I was too little to understand everything the preachers said, but I do remember one clear, spring morning a Reverend Howard spoke on how Abraham was the friend of God

(*see* James 2:23). *The friend of God*—that phrase
burned in my heart and made me wonder, even at that
young age, if there was any way I could find this God
who cares so much about man that He wants to be his
friend.

I guess you might say I became an apron-strings
child, because I always had to have Mom near me.
One day she slipped outside. I ran out the back door
and found her among some palm trees. She was fan-
ning herself with a big hat she always wore, and when
I finally caught up to her, she knelt down and began to
pray.

"Lord, take care of my baby, my son," she said. I
bowed my head, too, overwhelmed because she
thought so much of me that she actually mentioned me
to God.

But I didn't realize how deeply concerned my
mother was about me during that tender moment, for
she knew something I didn't know—she was suffering
from bone cancer. Over the following months she became weaker and less active, and I found I had to learn
to get along without my closest friend. The less time I
spent in her comforting presence, the more sharply I
sensed the tensions among the thirteen children in our
family.

The racial tensions that have so deeply troubled the
South were present right in our family, because some
of my mother's children were black, and others were
white. The white kids fit easily into the white community in Columbus. When we went downtown to a
movie, we had to separate and sit in different sections
of the theater because of segregation. Also, money always seemed to come from somewhere to provide
pretty cotton dresses for my older white sisters, while
most of my clothes were made out of flour bags, and
the only time I wore shoes was on Sundays.

But the racial problems in my family receded into
insignificance as my mother's health got worse. When

I was about eleven years old, she was confined to her bed. Then one rainy, stormy morning—before dawn had lightened the gloom—one of my sisters came into my room and woke me up.

"Mother wants to see you," she whispered urgently.

Dazed with sleep, I hurried to her bedside, where the rest of the family had gathered. But it was too late. She was already dead.

I had never seen a dead person before, so I didn't realize at first what had happened. I didn't know what it meant to die. For the next twenty-four hours, I must have been in a state of shock. I only remember pieces of the conversations and movements that went on around me.

I remember one of my sisters telling me that it was my fault—that I had worried my mother to death because I was sick all the time. That accusation burned deep into my heart, and I never forgot it. I knew my mother had worked very hard taking care of me and my younger brothers and sister, and I could see that having to take care of the family all by herself had helped to drain her of her health and strength. But I had never considered that I might be the one most responsible for her sickness. I didn't see how I could have been the main problem, because she had always seemed to enjoy being with me, showing love to me. But that accusation stuck with me.

The fact that Mom was gone forever began to dawn on me the next day, and I became very depressed and afraid and cried for the first time. One of my sisters took me in temporarily as we waited for funeral arrangements, and she sent me on an errand that took me past our house, which had been locked up. All the old stories I'd heard about "haints" and witches came back to me. I recalled that somebody had said that the dead always come back to get you, and if you look over your shoulder, you can see them following you. That scared the daylights out of me, so I ran past our house and returned by a different way from the store.

The day for the funeral arrived—a beautiful Sunday morning. I can remember walking up to the casket and looking down at my mother. I didn't cry; I was still in a state of shock. I didn't even cry as we rode the seven miles across town to the cemetery. Everything seemed so unreal, so distant from the patch of grass where I was standing. Some of the men in the family covered up her coffin after the preacher said his words, ". . . ashes to ashes, and dust to dust. . . ." Then someone arranged the flowers on the grave, and it was over.

When my mother died, my own world died, too. I just existed. Tentatively, I tried to find love in my older sisters, but couldn't. I sat and listened as they argued about who would have to take care of me. Nobody wanted me—that was clear enough. It was only days after my mother's death, and I was already beginning to feel like a stranger in a great big world.

Only weeks before, I had rested comfortably in the presence of a compassionate woman who loved me dearly. I knew her only as a child knows an affectionate mother. I didn't know, and still don't know, what kind of life she lived. I don't know why I had so many brothers and sisters with different fathers and different skin colors. I won't even speculate on that, because I know that in her final years her life matched up with the Bible. If she had problems as a young woman, I know her life was straightened out by the time I knew her. I'm convinced she knew the Lord—was a friend of God, just like Abraham—and now lives with Him in heaven.

But I was the friend of no one. I was an orphan against the world, and I had no idea where my next meal or bed or kind word would come from.

3

School for Crime

After my mother's death, I bounced around for several years, from one relative's home to another. I was always an outsider. No one showed me love or made me a member of the family. Sometimes the resentment about my presence ran so deep that my adult guardians openly rejected me.

I never received any birthday presents. One relative, on a whim, decided to punish me by not giving me any Christmas presents, even though the other children in the family received bicycles and other expensive gifts. On another occasion, one of my elder sisters was talking to a neighbor as I played on the grass nearby.

"I thought Spencer was supposed to be your brother," the neighbor commented. "How come he's so dark-skinned, and you and your kids are white?"

"Oh, Spencer's not my brother," my sister replied quickly. "He's only a *half*-brother."

I didn't know what it meant to be a half-brother, but I did understand that she had said I wasn't her brother. I didn't fit in anywhere.

I finally ended up in New Jersey at the home of a relative named Marge. I sensed she wasn't particularly happy to have me around, but at age fourteen I had no choice. I needed a place to sleep and eat, and I knew how important it was that I get an education. I had resolved to become *somebody*—a person of importance, with an independent identity. I wasn't sure who I was or where I had come from, but I knew that no one was going out of his way to help me. I had to make my own way, so I began to set goals for myself. Having spent a lot of time in hospitals as a youngster with hepatitis, and having seen my mother deteriorate steadily with a serious illness, I resolved to become a doctor.

But when I told Marge about my ambition, she scoffed and said, "You're too dumb!"

When you hear things like that, it does something inside you. I was shattered. I didn't react to her scorn right away—I never do—but her words began to gnaw at me. Before I realized it, a tremendous wall of resentment, or bitterness, had built up within me. All the rejections and abuse I had suffered during the years since my mother's death came to a head, and I became a slave to my own self-doubts.

At school, I turned into a very touchy, disturbed boy. It took very little to draw me into fights. One day a student teased me by calling me "pork chop" and "porky pig"—I was short and stubby, and he was kidding me about the way I looked.

But I was in no condition to be kidded. I was depressed and felt the whole world was against me. So I said, "I'm going to cut you up!" In those days, my word became my bond. If I said I'd do something, I'd do it, without fail. I felt I couldn't afford to tell somebody anything and not follow through on my promise. Making good on a personal promise like that was the only thing that gave me a sense of dignity.

So we squared off, and sure enough, I grabbed a knife from one of the other kids and started slashing away. The blade caught the fellow on the arm and opened him up like a piece of meat. I got showered with blood, somebody separated us, and we ended up in court, where Marge had to pay a fine.

Needless to say, my fighting at school and getting into trouble with the police didn't help my situation at home. I had never been what you'd call a favorite, but now things seemed to get worse. I always felt that Marge's son, Sammy, who was several years my junior, got preferential treatment. He went to the movies, learned to play the piano, and wore nice clothing, while I was forced to cut wood, wash dishes and clothes, and in general do all the dirty jobs around the house. I even felt discriminated against at breakfast. Marge made me eat bland grits and oatmeal; Sammy, on the other hand, always got the more tasty cornflakes.

"Why can't I have cornflakes?" I asked.

"Because you're too big!" Marge snapped. I couldn't figure that out, because I had seen grown folks eating cornflakes.

I continued to get into fights at school regularly and suffered a seriously split lip and a skull fracture, among other injuries. The only person who came close to being my friend was little Sammy, and I began to look out for him in the same way that an overprotective father would care for his own child.

One day, Sammy got kicked by some white kids who were playing football in the school yard, and he came crying to me for help. I marched over to the leader of the kids, a boy named Mike. We had words and got into a fight. I managed to keep out of his grasp until he got tired, and then I tripped him, jumped on top, and started beating him in the head with a brick.

Suddenly, I heard some man shout, "Hey, you gonna let that little nigger beat you like that?"

That really sparked things. All the white kids started after me, and I had to run for my life. They chased me to my house, and I barely had time to jump over the fence and make it to the door. But I wasn't about to let them think they had the upper hand. I ran to the kitchen, grabbed a butcher knife, and headed back outside. Quite a crowd had gathered by this time. They started moving angrily toward me, but I held them off with my knife.

"I can't fight all of you," I yelled. "But I'll fight *you*," I said, pointing to a large boy who seemed to be the leader of the group, "if you think you're man enough to beat me!"

Before we could start swinging, Marge came

through the front door and pulled me back toward the house.

"Marge, I was helping Sammy . . . ." I started to explain, but she wasn't interested in listening to my side of the story. She just started slapping me around, and soon I found myself down at the police station. Luckily for me, the boy I had injured with the brick had been released from the hospital with only minor injuries, so I got off with a light punishment from the local court. But I wasn't ready to forget how Marge had humiliated me in front of that crowd.

Seething after we arrived home from the court, I told her, "Marge, I'm telling you the truth about that fight, but I don't care if you don't believe me. And I'll promise you this—someday I'm going to kill you!"

She looked at me with a stunned expression, and I was sort of surprised, myself. But my life had been building up to that. She represented everything that frustrated me, everything that I had learned to hate over the years. And now I was caught in a trap of my own making: My word was my bond. What I promised, I had to fulfill. That conviction was the only stable point in my life, the only thing that gave me meaning. In my mind the question had become not whether, but *when*, I would kill her.

I know Marge realized what was happening inside me, because she became deathly afraid. I slept right across the hall from her, and she quickly put locks on all her bedroom doors and avoided me whenever possible. Then one day, she seemed almost too friendly when she said, "I'm worried about you because I don't think you're getting a very good education at the public school here. So I'm making other arrangements for you."

A few days later, a man came to the house to talk with me and said he was going to see that I would get into "a special school" so I'd be able to progress more rapidly in my studies. I liked the idea of getting a good education, because I still wanted to become a doctor.

But I felt something was wrong.

Soon I found myself standing before a judge again, who told me I would be going to a state residential school. I submitted quietly, because I still had high hopes about furthering my education. But the moment I passed through the front door, I knew I was not in any school! They gave me a number and assigned me to a section where some other tough boys were waiting to greet me with knowing smiles. I had been committed to a reformatory that was anything but an educational institution.

One of the boys in the dormitory section where I had been assigned immediately seemed overfriendly. He used words I didn't understand at first, but his meaning became clear when he said, giving me a too-affectionate pat, "I want you to be my girl friend 'cause you're nice."

Furious, I lit into the guy with fists and feet, and a couple of the "cottage fathers," or adult guards, had to rush in to pull me off. One of the cottage fathers, a big fat man, seemed to take great pleasure in beating both of us up. Then he made me kneel in a corner and say the "Hail Mary." I hadn't grown up as a Catholic, so I didn't know the words, and every time I made a mistake, he would step on my ankles. At first, I screamed and hollered from the pain, but I soon learned to grit my teeth and keep my mouth shut, because every time I yelled, he butted my head up against the concrete wall.

I was burning inside, on fire with rage against Marge and the guard. I resolved I would strike out against both of them someday. In the meantime, I had to bide my time and endure the pain, like some caged animal who lives only to destroy his cruel, tormenting captors.

I had heard that some of the cottage fathers committed homosexual acts with the boys, but perhaps they left me alone because I was a violent troublemaker. Of course, they probably could have beaten me into submission, but no one wanted to bother with me any more than necessary.

Contrary to what I had been told about improving my knowledge at this institution, there was no conventional education to speak of. The main source of instruction was the series of crime movies they allowed us to see. By studying Humphrey Bogart, Jimmy Cagney, and the other Hollywood tough guys that seemed to dominate our weekly film fare, I began to get ideas about how to break the law—how to cheat, steal, and kill—without getting caught.

I spent two years at this reformatory, and steadily got more hardened as a savvy prisoner and aspiring criminal. Most of my days were spent at hard labor— breaking ice in the winter, shoveling coal, loading huge grain carts, breaking rocks and boulders, cutting trees. If I tipped anything over or moved too slowly to suit the guards, I'd get rapped around or put into solitary confinement. It seemed I spent most of my time locked up in a separate room, rather than in the dormitory with the rest of the guys.

Finally, after two years and some months, I was released. I was seventeen years old and knew nothing but the life of a prisoner. At first, I thought I could fit into the world of a public-school student, and Marge reluctantly agreed to give me another chance in her home. But when I tried to mix with the other kids, I was labeled a jailbird. They knew where I had spent the past two years, and their parents wouldn't let them associate with me. It was like having leprosy— everyone kept away to avoid getting hurt or contaminated.

This treatment deepened my bitterness, and I ran away, only to be brought back by my parole officers. The very fact that I was on parole was a constant reminder to me that I hadn't been in any special school. No, I had been in jail, and there was no way to escape the fact. The parole officer decided to put me to work in a nursing home in a city where I didn't know my way around. I guess they figured it would be harder for me to escape from a place like that. I had to wash dishes, clean up the beds and rooms after sick or incontinent patients had messed them up, and help clean out the septic tank. Finally, after another two years, I decided I couldn't take that kind of life any longer, so I up and left.

I slept wherever I could find a likely place, and sometimes that meant a vacant building or outdoors on the grass near a river. I had to steal to eat. One of my techniques was to slip into a home for blind people and take money they left lying around in their rooms. I had no sympathy for blind people because I thought that, for the most part, they were phonies who were trying to get something for nothing by pretending they had a disability.

One evening, when I was especially hungry, I noticed a sign on a restaurant: DISHWASHER WANTED, and decided to try one final time to go straight. I walked in, applied for the job, and to my surprise, was hired. But then the woman who owned the place came in. She recognized me from my old hometown, where I had built up quite a reputation as a budding criminal.

"Get that thief out of here!" she screamed.

I tried to explain that I wanted to do honest work, but she wouldn't listen. She wouldn't even pay me for the day's work I had done. So I rushed out of the door, steaming with embarrassment and anger, so hungry I could hardly think straight. It was at that moment that I passed some garbage cans and spied an object that would change my entire life. It was a small toy gun, but it looked so real that, for a moment, even I was fooled into thinking it was genuine.

I picked it up and turned it over in my hands, thinking all the time about the possibilities that were opening up for me. Then I saw a taxi heading toward me and made up my mind. I flagged him down, and as he pulled over to the curb, I ran quickly toward the dark destiny that life seemed to be holding in readiness for me.

4

Confessions of an Outlaw

I climbed into the cab and directed the driver to take me to a small village a number of miles away. He said he didn't know the way, so I gave him instructions, making sure he went through one of the most deserted streets in town. When it was clear no other cars or pedestrians were around, I pulled my toy gun on the driver and told him to pull over to the curb and give me all his money.

He looked upset and nervous, and I wasn't feeling too calm myself, but I managed to get about seventy dollars from him before I pushed open the door and ran down the street. Unfortunately, I hadn't thought through my escape plan. I was in a strange part of town and had no idea where I could find a temporary hiding place.

I wandered around until I found a bridge that seemed to be the focal point of some traffic. The smartest thing to do, I decided, would be to lose myself in a crowd, so I started walking across the bridge. I noticed some policemen on the other side were stopping every car and questioning the drivers. Suddenly, it dawned on me that I might be the object of their search, so I knelt down on the bridge as though I were tying my shoelace and in the same motion tossed my toy gun into the river.

It wasn't a moment too soon, because I heard one of the cops shout, "There he is!" and out of the corner of my eye, I saw him sprinting toward me.

Without a word, this big policeman rushed up to me and hit me right in the mouth with a fist armed with a huge ring. As I tried to clear my head from the blow, he hustled me over to a patrol car and drove me directly to the nearest station house.

"You're in big trouble," he said, as we sped toward the police station. I just grunted, because I wasn't in the mood for conversation.

"Yeah, you almost killed a man," he continued, and now he had my attention.

"What do you mean?" I asked.

"That guy you robbed—he had a heart attack and almost died. He's in the hospital now, and they think he'll be okay. But you're still in trouble, and you better hope and pray he recovers. We got a witness, too, a man who saw you hanging around where the guy was robbed."

I lapsed into silence, but the cop had even more to say after I had been booked, because he learned I had been in trouble with the police before. "Too bad for you—that record you've got," he gloated. "You'll be treading the river for a few years, I imagine. Yeah, they'll send you up for a long time, now."

His prediction was all too accurate. I was indicted and convicted of armed robbery. The judge sentenced me to an indeterminate term at hard labor at a reformatory in the northern part of the state. The harassment and torture I had experienced at the earlier "school for crime" continued on an even grander scale, and my uncooperative attitude made a bad situation even worse.

Sometimes the guards would make me do pushups until I thought my arms would drop off. Then I'd have to stand up for eight hours straight, just watching a clock. The anger grew hotter and hotter inside me, until I felt like a volcano that needed only a slight disturbance to trigger a violent explosion.

That moment came while I was walking outside in formation with several other prisoners. A guard shouted at me, "You ain't marching in step!"

"I *am* marching in step!" I spat back defiantly.

He pulled me out of the line and said, "I'm going to write you up for insubordination."

"I don't care," I retorted, and that was all he needed.

He slapped me, and I hit him back, all my bottled-up fury erupting in that one punch. I didn't hit him squarely, and he started crawling all over me, punching, kicking until we fell to the ground in a tangle of arms and legs.

All that little show of protest got me was a badly cut mouth and thirty days in solitary confinement. There were no windows in my cell, and I had to exist on bread and water, except for a little decent food every third day—apparently to be sure I kept alive.

I could never accept the authority of the prison officials. I always felt that I had to argue with them, demand reasons for things they told me to do, strike back when they abused me in some way. As a result, I stayed in the "hole," or solitary confinement, more than anyone else I knew.

When I was out of solitary, I always seemed to draw the toughest work details—shoveling coal, digging on rocky ground with a pick. From walking on the rocks and rough ground, on the bottoms of my feet I developed deep scars and blisters that wouldn't heal. My feet were permanently damaged from the work, and I found I could only stand on them for a couple of hours before the terrible pain forced me to sit down.

Even when I was out of solitary confinement, there was little relief in returning to my cell at night, because most of the time the officials kept me in a maximum-security cottage. That meant I had to be locked in my room whenever I wasn't working, and I wasn't allowed the coffee, cigarettes, and other small privileges that made the lives of other prisoners bearable.

The only thing I could do during my nonworking hours was to think—and my thoughts invariably turned to revenge. These thoughts centered on Marge and the fact that I hadn't found the right moment to pay her back while I had been out on parole. Perhaps down deep I had hoped I might be able to escape my criminal background and make something decent of myself. But now, all thoughts of going straight seemed absurd, and I blamed her for ruining my life by sending me to that first school.

I was finally paroled again after spending my two full years in the reformatory, and this time I was assigned to stay with one of my sisters and her husband. Since Marge wasn't within my reach, I temporarily shelved my plans to get her. I was twenty years old, and had done nothing constructive with my life, so I decided to try the army. I applied, took all the entrance tests, and then returned a couple of weeks later to find out how I had done.

"Sorry, but we can't use you," the recruiter said. "You've got a bad police record."

There it was again—my bad background. It didn't seem that I could ever escape it. I went to a reunion of several of my brothers and sisters, but they all treated me like the black sheep of the family. That really upset me, and I decided, "Shucks, what's the sense of bothering with my folks at all? I'll find some other friends."

So I started hanging around a local poolroom and began to play cards, drink, and gamble. I had rented a little room near the pool hall and did some odd jobs cleaning buildings and summer resorts, but I wasn't making enough money to keep up the style of life I had chosen.

A snub-nosed .38 pistol helped me make up the difference. I started carrying it wherever I went, and it made me feel important. I had always wanted to be somebody, and even though I hadn't become the doctor or private investigator I had always dreamed about, still, I *was* somebody with that weapon in my pocket.

The guys I played cards with thought I had a good job, because I thought nothing of making big bets as we played Coon King and Skin and a lot of other fast games. What they didn't know was that I regularly robbed people by breaking into their homes or stealing their money from them by force on the streets. The stolen money enabled me to keep playing for high stakes, and I soon became a cardsharp who won either by skillful cheating or by bullying my way through when I got caught. Most of the people who played with me in my favorite bars and poolrooms knew I wasn't the arguing type, so if a dispute about my card tactics arose, they usually backed down.

For the first time in my life, I began to drink heavily, and soon the liquor got the best of me. One night I downed a whole bottle of wine, got sick, and passed out on the floor of the poolroom. Someone called my sister, and she and her husband came over, carried me back to their home, and deposited me half-dressed in their bathtub. I woke up the next morning with a cigar drooping out of my mouth and a splitting headache.

"This is no way to live!" I thought as I shuffled around the house, still half-dazed from my hangover.

I knew my life was falling apart, and I resolved to make one last effort to do something about it. The only good thing that I could recall ever happening to me was the love my mother had shown for me. As my mind wandered back over those sunny days we had spent together in church down in Mississippi, I decided to try to recapture some of that compassion and personal acceptance.

I had noticed a church down the street, and since it was Sunday morning, I decided to attend the services. With my dirty, rumpled clothes and unshaven face, I looked like a bum as I walked up to the doors of that church. But somehow I expected the congregation to accept me, as my mother had accepted me, because they held themselves out as people who were able to show the light and love of Christ to the world.

But I was disappointed. The ushers took one look at me and acted as though they had seen a ghost. They grabbed me as I started to walk down the aisle and rushed me to a back pew. Many of the church members who glanced in my direction shot me sour looks of distaste and rejection. Nobody—not one of these so-called Christians—gave me a kind word or offered to share with me the love that they sang about in their hymns, or that their preacher expounded upon in the pulpit that morning.

Crushed, I walked out before the service was over, but I made a note of the location of a Bible I had seen in one of the pews. "If they won't tell me about this God of theirs, maybe I'll just find out for myself," I thought. So that evening I broke into the church and stole the Bible. When I got back to my room with it, I couldn't understand a thing I read.

Years later, in reflecting on this incident, I wrote a poem in the form of a letter to that congregation, summing up the feelings that were tearing me apart that Sunday morning:

Dear Christians, I came to your church yesterday,
Hoping to find eternal life and peace of mind.
I came and went unnoticed,
Because you ignored my kind.
My clothes were torn and dirty,
My eyes bloodshot from hard liquors and wine,
For I had heard about your Savior
And wanted to make Him mine.
I watched you form your social cliques
To talk about your wealth and gold;
Not once did I hear you express
A burden for lost souls!
I observed you leave your church,
Ignoring me as you passed by,
And with a look of disgust and deep contempt,
You even cast at me an evil eye.
I stood on your church steps,
With my shoes worn far beyond repair,
Greatly bewildered that for lost souls,
You Christians showed no concern or care!
You talked much about the Son of God,
Whom you do not seem to know;

You spend millions of dollars on your church build-
   ings
And completely ignore the lost and spiritually
   poor.
By the time you receive this letter,
I may be forever lost in hell;
I wonder how many millions will join me there,
Because the love of Christ for a dying world,
You have failed to show and tell!

Abandoning the church and Christianity as failing to
provide an answer to my problems, I headed back into
the life of the committed criminal. I continued to hold
up people on the streets and break into their homes so
that I could get enough money for drinking and gambling. I was so far along the road to alcoholism that I
finally sold the main tool of my trade of armed
robbery—my .38 special pistol—to get a couple of bottles of booze. I soon degenerated to the point that I
began to "nickle-dime" bottles of cheap wine. In other
words, I would hang around bars and collect the last
drops from used bottles so that I could get a good swal-
low.

So oblivious to the outside world had I become that
I didn't have an inkling that I was the subject of a
police investigation until a couple of cops with a war-
rant for my arrest came to a poolroom where I was
hanging out. They said they had found my prints at a
couple of places where crimes had been committed.

The police charged me with breaking and entering a
summer home. I had broken in and stolen a number of
things, including an expensive ring that I hadn't been
able to sell, because it was too hot. The police found
the ring on me, and with the footprints and finger-
prints, I knew I didn't have a chance in court.

But the cops who arrested me weren't content with
their evidence and the punishment they knew I would
get from the legal system. They decided to mete out a
little justice of their own when they got me alone in

the station house. One of the guys punched me repeatedly in the belly, while the other banged my head against the wall. They kept asking me questions and, dissatisfied with my answers, they kicked and slapped me so hard that my head began to ring. They must have sensed that I was on the verge of fighting back, because they started showering me with abusive language and threats and beat me even harder with their fists.

I was known as a troublemaker in town, and I suppose I should have expected this kind of treatment, but I could hardly contain my fury. At that moment I became a vicious cop hater. The hatred that I had harbored before ballooned into a bitterness that encompassed these policemen as well. I would get them all, I resolved. I wouldn't rest until they were dead. I wanted to see them die, painfully, by my own hand, just as they had forced me to live painfully by theirs.

The nightmare that I had been living got worse and worse: the fight in the county jail over the cigarettes I had won in a card game; my decision to burn the mattress to get the attention of the jail guards; their retaliation by committing me to an institution for the criminally insane; the tortures of an isolation cell and chemical-therapy attacks on my brain.

As I lay on the cold floor of that insane-asylum cell, freezing from the cold that was torturing my naked body, and burning inside from the feelings of humiliation and rejection, the only thing I had to live for was revenge. I vowed that I would kill everyone who had abused me, and I wouldn't hesitate any longer about carrying out my promise. "My word is my bond," I kept repeating to myself. That was the only idea, the only conviction that gave my life meaning. I knew I had to act on it or give up any right to live at all. But years in prison lay ahead of me before I would have the opportunity to fulfill my demonic purpose in life.

5

In Chains

After three months in the isolation cell at the hospital for the criminally insane, I was finally sent before a board of psychiatrists, who asked me question after question about my background and attitudes toward life. They sent me away, deliberated on my case, called me back, and announced, "We've found that you're not insane, even though you are a vicious and violent person. You'll be returned to court to stand trial on the charges against you."

Despite the fact that I was still behind bars, I almost felt like a free man. I had made it out of the crazy house with my mind still intact—without the destructive treatments like shock therapy and lobotomies that I had feared would be used to devastate my brain. But my sense of liberation was short-lived. I was convicted on the breaking-and-entering charge and sentenced to hard labor at still another reformatory.

My first assignment was to do outdoor work—breaking rocks with a sledgehammer, moving the rocks hundreds of yards in a wheelbarrow to a distant location, then hauling them back to the original starting point. It was meaningless labor, and my scarred feet, which had healed somewhat while I had been outside the prison, acted up again. The blisters and bruises got so bad that I could hardly walk, so the prison officials transferred me inside, to the laundry room.

That was a much better job for my tender feet, and I worked hard and well there for a time. But I couldn't seem to keep out of trouble. Another inmate got mad at me and pushed me into a hot pressing machine, and I burned myself. Enraged, I jumped him, and we got into a fight. The authorities threw me into the hole on bread and water for ten days, and then denied me parole and ordered me to go back outside to work. Because I knew I'd never be able to take the rough walking, I refused.

"We think you're goldbricking, but we'll give you a week to think about it—either you obey us, or else," they said.

But I still refused, so they transferred me to a state prison. The conditions there were much worse and the restrictions on inmates more severe than at the last reformatory—especially for me, since I was immediately assigned to the maximum-security wing. Within a month, I was already in trouble. I was served some food I didn't like in the mess hall, and told one of the guards, "I'm not going to eat that!"

You don't talk like that to officials in prisons, but it seemed I'd never learn. The guard told me to report to the Center, which was the headquarters that coordinated prisoner affairs, and they wrote me up for disobeying an order. My punishment was to spend five days in the hole on bread and water. "You're starting off on the wrong foot around here," they warned. But I wasn't in the mood to listen.

Shortly after I was released from solitary, I talked back to another guard, cursing at him and telling him I didn't care whether he beat me or not. He took up my challenge and beat me to the floor with his club. These guards represented cops to me—especially the two cops who had beaten me after my breaking-and-entering arrest.

By this time, my hatred knew no bounds. I had been confined to my cell indefinitely and was allowed out only to work, eat, and attend church services. Since I didn't choose to go to church, I had plenty of time to wallow in my anger and resentment, and to plot how I would take revenge on my growing list of enemies.

I got tired of hating and fell into a deep depression as I heard the other prisoners laughing and talking with one another and going to the movies together at night. Some people even seemed to find friends in this state prison, when I hadn't even been able to find one on the outside. The only friend I had known in recent years was that .38 caliber gun I had sold to buy a bottle of liquor.

What am I living for? I wondered. The answer that kept returning to my mind was, "Nothing." I was living for *nothing*, so why go on living at all? Why not just end it right now, by hanging myself with a bed sheet, or by slashing my wrists?

All the fears and uncertainties I had been suppressing for so many years surfaced. Trembling alone in my cell, I was gripped by a tremendous fear of dying. I knew I wanted to escape from my emotional and physical chains—and suicide seemed the easiest way. But I didn't want to die in my present condition, because I realized I might have to give account to someone, namely, to God. I had seen other men kill themselves in prison, and I envied them in a way, but I knew I had to make another effort to find out about that Supreme Being who had known Abraham as a friend.

Swallowing all my hostility and hatred, I resolved to give the church another chance and try attending one of those chapel services that I had avoided since being in solitary. It took a lot of courage to go to that service. I had the feeling that every guard and inmate who saw me was snickering, because the tough guy who was always defying authority was finally admitting he couldn't handle life all by himself.

But whatever answers I was expecting from that service didn't materialize. The preacher told a lot of pointless jokes and made me feel even more ridiculous than I had felt sitting in my hot, stuffy cell. The church had let me down again, and I returned to my cell more depressed than ever. Once again, my eyes fell on the bed sheet that could so easily be turned into a noose. *Was that the only way that I could find my freedom?*

6

Finally, Freedom

I stood at a major crossroads in my life. Almost anything—harsh words from a guard, one more unhappy thought—could have pushed me into suicide. But a combination of my own stubbornness and fear of death, and some unexplainable tugging from outside, made me want to try that chapel again.

Doggedly, I left my cell for the next chapel call, and this time I found myself listening to a friendly looking, stout layman named Jack Binns.

I was twenty-two years old at the time, and for the first time in my life I heard how much God loved me, personally. Mr. Binns was speaking about Acts 26, where the Apostle Paul stood before King Agrippa and told of his conversion. Paul declared that God could change the life of any man who repented of his sins and asked the Lord Jesus to come into his heart.

As I listened to the sermon, I realized that Paul had actually gone around killing the early Christians. I thought: *Lord, if You can forgive the Apostle Paul, who went around killing Your people, then You can forgive me, too! At least I've never killed anybody.*

Then Mr. Binns quoted Paul's words:

> To this day I have had the help that comes from God, and so I stand here testifying both to small and great, saying nothing but what the prophets and Moses said would come to pass.
>
> Acts 26:22 RSV

Lord, if You could save this man, Paul, I know that You can save me!

Almost as if he had heard my thoughts, Mr. Binns

quoted again from Acts 26, where Paul said: ". . . I would to God that not only you but also all who hear me this day might become such as I am—except for these chains" (v. 29 RSV).

Except for these chains—Paul had been imprisoned just as I was, yet he seemed to have a joy and inner freedom that I had never experienced. I wanted that eternal release, too!

Again as if in answer to my thoughts, Mr. Binns closed his message with an invitation. "Now I'd like for anybody who wants to accept Christ to raise his hand—right now!"

I didn't hesitate a moment. A new hope, a new life, had begun for me. My hand shot up into the air, almost of its own accord. After the service, Mr. Binns asked me to join him at the front of the chapel.

"Did you really mean it when you raised your hand?" he asked.

"Yes," I exclaimed, with a sense of total conviction now moving me. My heart had finally opened to the God of heaven, the friend of Abraham. I saw no rainbows, heard no thunder, but my heart was overwhelmed with love and joy, that God could actually *love* someone like Spencer Parker.

Mr. Binns handed me a copy of the Gospel of John and gave me assurance of my salvation by showing me several Scripture passages such as:

> But to all who received him, who believed in his name, he gave power to become children of God.
>
> John 1:12 RSV

"God has forever forgiven you, Spencer—you can be sure of that!" he said, and I felt the sun shine inside me for the first time since my mother had died.

"From this day on," I resolved, "I will serve the Lord, no matter what befalls me."

My life was like a dream for the next few hours. I walked out to the prison yard—I think that area was off limits to me, but miraculously, none of the guards challenged me—and I just strolled around, praising God. Even though I was soon released from solitary confinement, I still chose to spend time in my cell alone, so that I could pray and read the Bible. Every chance I'd get, I'd head back to my cell. Although, before, I had dreaded being alone in my cell with my suicidal thoughts, now I looked forward to the quiet time of meditation in the Word of God.

At first the prison officials thought I was a nut—refusing to see the evening films now that I had the opportunity. They sent me to see the prison psychiatrist, but he found nothing wrong with me. The old depressions and desire for revenge had miraculously disappeared.

Finally, I was free of the chains of self-doubt and hatred, and in their place was that complete liberty that can only come from divine love. God had really become my friend, and I found myself looking forward each day to knowing Him better.

It was in one of those peaceful, exhilarating moods that followed my conversion that I penned this poem, the first I ever wrote, by the dim light of my cell:

A mighty voice in heaven cried, that echoed to and fro;
It was the voice of God saying, "Who will go below?
"For man has grown tired of Me and chosen the way of sin,
"Who will go and die," asked God, "that man might live again?"
The angels all kept silent, and began to look around;
Then the King of Glory left His throne and laid aside His crown.
When God the Heavenly Father saw what the King of Glory had done,

He said, "I love so the world, I'll give my only
   Son."
The King of Glory said, "Father, I'll go and save
   the lost;
"I'll give my life a ransom up on the rugged
   cross. . . ."

The rest of this poem has been lost, and I can't remember the ending. It was misplaced or destroyed by
the prison guards who were making a routine search of
the cellblock for weapons, narcotics, and other con-
traband.

I'll never forget the feeling of inner peace that carried me through my last days in prison and into freedom when I was paroled a few months later. But my
problems weren't over, by any means. My experience
with the perfect love of God hadn't prepared me for
the imperfect love of other Christians, and the dangerous remnants of my own sinful nature.

7

The Conspiracy Within

My first home when I got out of the state prison was
a room on the top floor of a church. I had no idea what
it was like to be a Christian outside prison bars, so I
was looking forward to learning about how to conduct
myself and relate to other believers.

But the people I met in that church weren't willing
to accept me for what I was—a baby Christian, who
needed to be nurtured along slowly and lovingly in
the faith. Instead, they made me feel guilty by saying,

"You're not filled with the Holy Ghost. You've got to be filled with the Holy Ghost!"

I wanted to do the right thing, so one night I knelt down as they gathered around me, praying and screaming, "Jesus! Jesus!" Then somebody hit me on the neck so hard I thought they might break it, and they poured oil over my head. By this time I was completely confused, but they urged me, "Holler 'Jesus!' Holler 'Jesus!'" When I didn't holler, someone yelled, "Lord, loose him! Got a demon! Got a demon!"

Something about this experience didn't seem quite right for me, and the next day I felt ashamed, even a little dirty, and refused to say where I had been when a girl at a drugstore where I worked part time asked me what I had been doing.

I avoided meetings at the church after that, and I think the pastor of the congregation, a woman, resented me. But I continued to study the Bible, and I secretly began to harbor a desire to become a preacher and missionary to India. I had taken a couple of Bible courses through a correspondence school, and when I had some free time during the day and no one else was in the church, I would slip up into the pulpit and practice some sermons I had prepared.

One day I was standing up in that pulpit, speaking as though I had an entire congregation listening to me, when the pastor of the church walked through the door and saw me.

"Nobody can go into that pulpit!" she shouted. "That's a holy place!"

She rushed up and grabbed me, and I came close to hitting her. I've never liked to be touched in a hostile way, and my first reaction had always been to fight. It frightened me, when I realized what a temper I still had, but I managed to restrain myself. And I had no further chances to get into arguments with the pastor because she arranged to have me tossed out of my room in the church the next day.

But God was still with me. I managed not to become bitter at the treatment I had once again received from church members, and an elderly man—a real saint— stepped in as an answer to my prayers and offered me a room in his family home at a very low rent. I found a job washing dishes at a nearby restaurant that was owned by a very nice man named Jimmy, who allowed me to take extra food home at night. He and his wife knew I was poor, and they respected the fact that I was willing to work long, late hours whenever they needed me.

If I had been a more mature Christian, I might have avoided any more angry outbursts and unpleasant encounters with the law. But the old Spencer Parker was not quite dead, and he was always ready to take over my personality whenever an opportunity arose.

I had to work late one night and missed my bus, so I started walking home on those feet that had been injured from so much hard labor in prison. I made it about a mile up the road and decided I'd rest for a few minutes, but just as I stopped, a young man pulled his car to the side of the road near me and asked if I'd like a ride.

"Sure!" I said.

He replied, "Hop in!"

He drove me close to the town where I lived, and I told him, "Thanks, you can let me out here and I'll get a taxi."

Before I could get out, he said, "Don't you think you owe me something for the ride?"

"Well . . ." I started to reply, thinking he wanted money, but before I could answer he let me know in definite terms what it was he wanted. He said the least I could do was perform a homosexual act with him.

That request triggered a deep hatred I had developed for homosexuals. A rush of revolting memories flooded into my mind, of the way other inmates had tried to force their immoral attentions on me at various times in prison. Before I realized what I was doing, I flew into a rage, pulled out of my pocket a nail file that folded like a knife, and jammed it into the driver's throat so violently that I drew blood.

"I'll kill you. I swear I'm going to kill you!" I screamed. But I regained control of myself, jumped out of the car, slammed the door so hard I thought it would come right off the hinges, and took a taxi directly home.

My anger cooled down considerably as I sat in my room taking care of my sore feet, but it worried me that violence was still so near the surface of my personality. I felt justified in getting angry at the guy, but I knew I had overreacted. Christ, I could see, still had a lot of work to do in subduing the old man inside me.

Still mulling over the night's events, I walked around the corner to a little diner where I often had my supper. I hadn't even bothered to change from my white dishwasher's outfit, because it was so late and and I was so hungry. Just as I walked out of the restaurant, a police car passed me, stopped, and then backed up.

"Hey, come over here for a minute—we want to talk to you," one of the cops said. When I had joined them next to the car, he asked, "Why don't you tell us what you've been doing tonight?"

I recounted how I had worked late, started walking home and then caught a ride with the young man, whose name I gave them. "When we got to town, he asked me to commit this homosexual act with him, and I actually told the guy I was going to kill him." I pulled out my nail file, which still had blood on it, and showed it to them. I honestly didn't see anything legally wrong with what I had done.

But the police had heard enough. They made me get in the car with them and drove me down to headquarters. The first person I saw when I walked through the door was the young homosexual.

"That's him!" the fellow said, pointing a finger at me.

"That's him—what?" I retorted.

"You held me up!" he said.

The police actually had to hold me back, because by this time I was moving toward the guy with my fists clenched. "Man, you know I didn't rob you!" I shouted. "But you know why I cut you—because you asked me to commit a homosexual act! That's why I cut you, and I told you I'd kill you!"

"Did you rob this man?" one of the policemen asked me.

"No, officer. I work. I didn't rob this guy. Look—all I've got in my pocket is twelve dollars!"

But then they learned from their files that I had been in prison, and that did it. "Book him. We'll take him to trial," one cop said.

The seal was placed on my fate when I went in to be fingerprinted. The officer who did the fingerprinting was none other than the father of the young man who had given me the ride and was now accusing me of robbery.

"So you're the _____ that robbed my son!" he said. "One of these days, you're going to get a bullet in you!"

By now I knew I didn't have a chance, so I decided there was no sense in holding anything back. "I don't care how you react to what I say," I said to the cop. "But you should know—your son is a homosexual, and one day I'm going to prove it. My freedom is being taken away because that boy has turned around and accused me of robbing him. He knew he could deny what he asked me to do, because you're his father, and a law-enforcement officer. That's all the backing he needs."

The father shouted some profanity at me, and they sent me back to my cell. My lawyer wanted me to plead guilty, but I insisted on going to trial. As might be expected, I lost the case. During the sentencing procedure, my employer and several other character witnesses appeared on my behalf in an effort to keep me free, but that didn't move the judge. "This man is too dangerous to society," he said. "I won't let him remain a free man and endanger the lives of our decent citizens."

So I was sentenced to several more years in prison for an "armed robbery" I didn't commit. I didn't know how I was going to face the inmates and guards, who knew about my conversion and had learned to respect me for my change of life. After I was put in the local jail to await transfer to the state prison, I found my thoughts moving back over all that had happened to me in my life, and I started feeling bitter again. I recalled how badly I thought Marge had treated me; how those two cops had beaten me up after arresting me for breaking and entering; and how the homosexual had wrongfully accused me of armed robbery.

It seemed I couldn't stay out of trouble. One way or another, I was always hurting myself or getting hurt. My mind started working the way it had before I ever met Jesus Christ: *Okay*, I thought, *I'll go to prison. But when I come out, they're dead!* I became so enveloped in my own anger that I couldn't think of anything else. Although there was a Bible in my cell, I had no desire to read it. I spent all my time planning and scheming how to get even with those I felt had hurt me.

My thoughts of revenge were interrupted by a jeering voice from the cell next to mine: "Yeah, I know him! He's one of those jailhouse preachers! He's supposed to be a Christian!"

I looked over and saw Stan, a fellow I had known the first time I was in the state prison. He was bigger than I, and I was afraid of him, but his sneering, harassing voice soon got on my nerves. He didn't seem interested in doing anything except bother me, so I started planning how I would make him shut up.

Something inside me seemed to say, *When he comes out of his cell the same time you do, you hit him! And when he goes down, you step in his mouth!*

I dwelt on these thoughts, and the next time they let us out together, I released all the bitterness and frustration inside me. I hit him and he crashed against the bars. The blow had dazed him so that he couldn't get himself together, and I grabbed him in a headlock and began to pound his head against the bars. It took three men to pull me off him.

As I lay on my bunk later that day and thought about what had happened, I began to come to my senses. *I'm a Christian,* I thought. *Even though I'm in trouble again, I'm still a Christian. But now I'm making matters worse.* Then it hit me: *Wow, it's the devil! Man, I never realized how powerful he is.*

I immediately saw that only Satan could have given me the strength to do what I did to that man. Even though Stan was much bigger than I was, Satan had given me the power to handle him as though I were handling a feather. The devil was actually using me to discredit the name of the Lord Jesus Christ.

This insight helped me keep my temper when I was transferred back to the state prison to serve out my sentence. And believe me, I needed help! The guards and inmates who knew me from before were merciless in their abuse:

"Here comes the Rev! Hey, Rev, you got your Bible?"

"Hey, see who's back? Preacher Parker's back!"

"See, I told you, he ain't nothing but a jackleg preacher."

I knew I wasn't a jackleg preacher—a phony guy who uses the Word of God for his own profit—but there was no way to argue with them or explain what had happened to me. So I turned away from those scornful voices and relied on prayer, the major resource God had given me. I gathered the insights God gave me during those first trying days in prison in a poem, which I called "The Conspiracy Within"—

Dear Lord, You know the strong desires and will-
    ingness of my heart,
To live in the Holy Spirit, forever pleasing God.
Lord, You see the giant evils—self, Satan, and the
    world—at work deep within,
Together, they have conspired to enslave my soul
    to sin.
But by faith in Thee, O Lord, I resist and take my
    stand
Against this evil through Jesus Christ, the Son of
    God and man.
Dear Holy Spirit, will You take complete control of
    me?
Destroy, enslave everything that comest not from
    Thee;
And when these trials and evils come like a mighty
    flood,
Dear Lord, make haste, deliver me, and shield me
    with Thy blood.
These triune evils have conspired, Dear Lord, to
    make a ruin of me;
Their hope and aim is to disgrace the Christ of Cal-
    vary.
But if all the power of hell should press hard upon
    my soul;
I'm more than conqueror with Jesus Christ who
    keeps and makes me whole.
Yes, I'm fully persuaded and trust in Christ—I do
    believe
That He will not let me, by these evils, be over-
    come and deceived.
Dear Lord, when by Thy grace I have conquered
    the conspiracy at work within,
I'll praise Thee for causing me to triumph victori-
    ously in the end!

8

My Family Found

The spiritual healing that took place inside me during those first few weeks in prison was a slow process. I knew God had told me, through the Apostle Paul:

> No temptation has overtaken you that is not common to man. God is faithful, and he will not let you be tempted beyond your strength, but with the temptation will also provide the way of escape, that you may be able to endure it.

> 1 Corinthians 10:13 RSV

Still, it was hard, listening to those guards sneering as they walked past my cell, "What happened to your Bible, Rev?" My life had become lopsided. I wanted to hate, yet I didn't want to hate. When I tried to pray, the homosexual who had lied about me came before my mind, just like I was switching on a TV set. He was standing there, mocking me, just like the guards.

Then, for the first time in my life, ordinary Christians began to reach out, to encourage me, to nurture me. My prison chaplain, the Reverend Stewart A. Snedeker, came over to see me regularly and to pray with me, to encourage me in the Lord. He really believed I was innocent of that crime, just as I *knew* I was innocent. I started pouring out my feelings to Reverend Snedeker in a way that I never could before. I told him honestly that I planned to be good so that I could hurry up and get out and take revenge on my enemies.

But the chaplain never condemned me, never said, "No that's wrong—you're evil, to have thoughts like that!" He just nursed me along, through the Word of God. He acted like a doctor who knew his patient, a spiritual physician who was dealing tenderly with a sorely damaged soul.

Gradually, this man brought me back to a state of reasonably good spiritual health. I found I was able to take strong giant steps in the Lord, with less wavering. I could respect authority, and ignore the jeers, which had become less frequent as time passed. The Lord *was* providing me with a way of escape. And the secret to my recovery, I learned, was in the Bible: "Therefore confess your sins to one another, and pray for one another, that you may be healed" (James 5:16 RSV).

Occasionally, though, those old feelings of revenge would still crop up in my mind. I was sitting at a table one day, feeling rather upset about that guy who had lied to have me put back in prison. An older Christian inmate walked over and sat down beside me.

"Hey, Spence, what's the matter?" he asked. "You look so melancholy today."

"Yes, this bothers me," I said, looking down at my hands. "I just got to get even with that fellow."

"Look, you used to fight, didn't you?" he asked.

"Yeah."

"When you got knocked down, what made you aware you didn't have to stay down?"

"When I got up," I answered, unsure where he was leading me.

"Everybody falls sometime in life," he explained. "But everybody doesn't have to stay down! If you want to stay down, I have nothing more to say. If you want to get up, we'll have fellowship."

I went back to my cell and thought about what that prisoner had told me. He, the other Christian inmates, and the chaplain had sheltered me through these hard times. None of them asked what I had done to be back in prison. They had heard plenty of rumors and seen the newspapers about my arrest, but they didn't probe me for details. They just accepted me. They had committed murder, grand larceny, and drug offenses, but God had changed them, just as He was changing me.

For the first time in my life, I had found a family—a spiritual family of committed Christians, who really wanted to support me and to love me.

I think my need for revenge left me for good at that moment, as I realized I had to start looking forward into the light, rather than backward into the darkness. I had confessed my sins, as God had commanded, and His promise to "forgive us our sins, and cleanse us from all unrighteousness" (1 John 1:9) had become a reality in my life.

Now that I was free inside, I could have complete fellowship with Chaplain Snedeker and my other Christian friends. Each had a verse of consolation from the Scriptures for me when it seemed I might stumble. As a father helps his little kid through childhood, so they nursed me in the faith, until finally I was able to walk boldly on my own again.

Soon I had impressed the prison officials so well with my good conduct that I was sent to honor camp, under minimum security. Then I came up for parole, and everyone was certain I'd get it. Sure enough, the parole board granted me my freedom, on the condition I could get someone on the outside to sponsor me. Excited, I immediately got in touch with members of my family. But nobody wanted me. They had heard about my going back to prison after becoming a Christian, and they weren't willing to take a chance on me. "It's the worst thing, Spencer, not to live up to what you profess," one of them told me condescendingly.

So I was stuck in prison because no one on the outside believed in me! As far as they were concerned, I was irretrievably lost—even though I knew in my heart that Jesus had found me and made me completely His. The prison officials gave me all sorts of privileges, but that didn't stop the months and years from slipping by. My brothers in Christ inside the prison walls joined me in praying for my freedom, but for a long time the only answer the Lord seemed to be giving me was "Wait."

So I waited and prayed and shared my concern with other believers. Then one day, an elderly gentleman in his early seventies—Mr. Ernest Chase—made one of his regular visits to the prison farm where I was confined. He was a businessman who felt God had called him to minister to prisoners, and he listened intently as I told him about my problems in securing my freedom.

"I don't know what help I can be, Spencer, but I promise you this—I'll pray about it!" he said. I thanked him, expecting I'd probably never hear from him again.

But he wrote me a few days later and said, "I believe the Lord wants you to come and stay with me and my wife, Spencer, so I'm going to write your parole board."

I could hardly believe what I was reading, so I went over the letter carefully once again. The Lord had finally answered all those prayers we had been sending to Him! The parole board soon got in touch with me and said they would honor Mr. Chase's request and release me to his custody. Shortly afterwards, in July of 1961, I was on a train to Newark, New Jersey, free for the first time in nearly five years.

When I got off that train, Mr. Chase was waiting for me, and he rushed over with a big smile and put his arms around me. It was hard for me to believe this was happening. It was the first time in my twenty-eight years that I'd been met at a train station by anyone other than a cop. And this time, there was no jail cell waiting for me. Mr. Chase drove me to his home in Montclair, a huge mansion, surrounded by trees, shrubbery, and a swimming pool. Mr. Chase's wife, Hazel, met us at the door with open arms. It was as though they were welcoming a long-lost son back home.

I've never been able to get over the generosity of Mr. and Mrs. Chase. Here was a couple—total strang-

ers to me—whom God used to help me in spite of my
past. They knew about the crimes I had committed.
They knew I had been in an institution for the criminally insane. I learned later that the parole board had
advised them against taking me because of my
psychiatric history. Yet they gathered me into their
arms and comforted me.

With his gnarled hand on my arm, he looked over at
me as we were eating lunch and said, "I had a son
once, but he was drowned. Now, *you're* my son."

I could hardly hold back the tears.

Here was a man who was doing what the Bible says
to do. I was so caught up in awe and admiration that I
hardly heard what he told me as he showed me around
the house. I felt as though I were dreaming as he
ushered me into my own quarters, where I had a bath-
room, kitchen, lounge, and spacious windows that
overlooked his wooded grounds. Tentatively, I sat
down on the soft bed. For the first time in my life, I
would have a decent place to sleep. In the past, my
head had rested, more often than not, on a floor, or cold
concrete or a dirty straw mattress.

"This is yours, Spencer," he said, gesturing at the
quarters he had given me. "Just make yourself at
home, and don't worry. We understand, and we just
want to help you."

All I could reply was, "Hey, this is like a dream—this
is like a dream."

The Chases introduced me to their son-in-law, who
was with the Atomic Energy Commission, to their
daughter, and to their other relatives and friends.
Everywhere I went, I was accepted as a member of
their family. Mr. Chase arranged for me to get a job on
the maintenance crew of a nearby hospital, and I soon
started witnessing to people there, telling them about
how Christ had changed my life.

"Hey, Spence, why don't you start a prayer meeting,
or Bible class, or something like that around here?"
somebody asked one day.

"Do we have a chapel?" I replied.

There was a chapel in the building, and I began to teach a Bible-study class there every morning before work. Ever since my conversion, I had experienced this nagging feeling that I should become a foreign missionary, and I had studied the Bible through correspondence courses with that end in mind. But one day as I was working in that hospital, the Lord seemed to speak to me in my heart: "Open your eyes and look around you, Spencer," He seemed to be saying. "You have plenty of miserable people living right next to you."

My eyes seemed to see for the first time, as I looked at the deep problems of sin in my own neighborhood. I said, "Lord, forgive me. Whatever You want, I'll do it right here." And He continued to open up doors, like that Bible class and others in the community, so that I could expand my ministry as a layman.

Of course, my way wasn't always easy in those first years, as I adjusted to life outside prison walls. I seriously injured my hand in an explosion of hot tar at the hospital, and that accident put me on permanent disability compensation for several years. Then Mr. Chase gave me a new car as a gift, and while I was on a trip, another driver crashed into me and totaled the car and seriously injured my back. But my faith was growing stronger all the time, and I found I could let the Lord have His way in these matters. I concentrated more intensely on several Bible studies I was leading, and I asked my fellow Christians to pray with me that God would give me the greatest gift that I could imagine—a wife modeled after the good wife of Proverbs 31.

For six long years, beginning with my last year in prison, I had prayed God would give me a wife. I desperately wanted my marriage to be the kind of marriage He wanted. During this period, I met a couple of girls I thought the Lord wanted me to marry, but it turned out He didn't. The father of one of them said he didn't want to be bothered with a West Indian in his family.

But even though it seemed God was turning a deaf ear to my prayers, things that I was not even vaguely aware of were beginning to happen. In the very year I started praying for a wife—1960—a young woman named Virginia Holmes began to read the Bible seriously. She became the organist at a church where Tom Skinner, the evangelist, conducted a series of meetings in 1962. I was present at one of those meetings when she responded to his invitation to salvation.

Virginia didn't come forward when Skinner first issued the altar call. But at the very end he said, "I know you're struggling, but right there in that seat you can ask Jesus to come into your heart. Just ask Him! Tell Him you will!"

Virginia felt a tremendous release inside her at that moment, and she went downstairs after the service to learn how she could be assured of her salvation. Within a few weeks, she was attending one of my Bible studies, listening to my prayer requests for the "good wife" of Proverbs 31.

At first, I really think she felt sorry for me. To cheer me up, she started writing me notes and happy-birthday cards. We began to talk a lot together at the Bible class, and finally I invited her out to eat with me. What I failed to tell her, though, was that I had also asked four other sisters to join us. I think she may have been a little disconcerted, piling into the car with all those other women, but she didn't complain at all about it.

Then one night I was driving home from a prayer meeting by myself, and I began to pray: "Lord, I'm lonely. I want to get married. If You don't help me, I'm afraid I'll end up sinning against You. Please help me out!" And suddenly it hit me—why not ask Virginia? She seemed perfect for me, and I had learned to care very much for her.

Afraid I couldn't say everything I wanted to say in

one conversation, I decided to put my thoughts down in a letter. I told her I felt the Lord was moving me to write to her to propose marriage, and I explained why I felt we were right for each other. I also told her I'd talk to her later in person. But when Virginia received the letter, she thought I was joking, so she told some people, "Spencer's just trying to be smart—I know him!"

About two or three weeks went by before I saw her again, because I wasn't able to make it to the Bible studies we both attended. But when we finally ran into each other, she invited me over to dinner and said, "Look, I'm curious about that letter. What did you mean by that?"

"Oh, I did intend to talk to you about that," I said. "I wanted you to have everything on paper, so you could read it again and think about it. You see, I feel the Lord is leading us into marriage."

She seemed dumbfounded.

"But I want you to be sure you have your communication signals clear from the Lord," I hastened to add. "Why don't you go home and pray about it? I have no doubts whatsoever that the Lord has called us to be husband and wife. I can wait as long as I have to, but I want you to be sure. So you ask the Lord about it."

I was out the next morning, but when I got back home, I found a message saying Virginia had called. She said she'd be coming by my place later that morning, and I was sitting on the porch when she arrived.

"It's true," she said, smiling as she got out of her car.

"What's true?"

"The Lord confirmed it!"

"Confirmed what?" I asked.

"That we're to be married!" she replied, half-excited and half-annoyed at me by now.

"That's good," I said casually.

"Oh, here! How about getting us some hamburgers!" she said.

When I got to the restaurant, it finally dawned on me

what had happened. *Wow!* I thought to myself, and I'm sure everyone near me was staring at the expression on my face. I always have a delayed reaction to things—even something as important as my own engagement. But now the full impact of what Virginia had said hit me. She was going to become my wife! My loneliness was over! My prayers had been answered! The "good wife" of Proverbs 31 was to be mine!

We were married in February of 1966, and about five hundred people attended our wedding. Within a few years, we had two wonderful daughters, Naomi and Ruth. And finally, the last of my dreams—to be a full-time Christian worker—came to pass. I had managed to finish high school and had completed many college-level Bible courses, but my goal to make my living and devote all my waking hours to the spreading of the Gospel had somehow eluded me.

But, according to God's timetable, not my own, those prayers were finally answered, too, when the Pocket Testament League asked me to join them as a staff member. They distribute the Word of God throughout the world, and my mission, at first, was to work with prisoners who didn't know the love of Christ.

Then God placed a deep compassion in my heart for the very men who had once been my worst enemies—policemen. Where I had once hated cops, now I felt a growing burden to approach them with the Gospel. So with the PTL's blessing, I began to visit organizations of Christian policemen. As a missionary with the Pocket Testament League, I was able to distribute Gospels of John and entire New Testaments to people in all walks of life: to people in the inner city, to people in suburbia, to those in prisons, to policemen, to all who would accept a portion of God's Word.

One day I received a call from Deputy Police Chief Jack Dougherty, of Bloomfield, New Jersey. He told me he belonged to the Northern New Jersey Fellowship of Christian Lawmen, and he was wondering if I would like to visit them for a breakfast meeting. I accepted, and while attending the gathering, I gave them my testimony. I told them in detail about how I had become a cop hater; how I had spent most of my life in prison planning how to kill policemen; and how I had finally undergone a complete change of heart by committing myself to Jesus Christ.

Their response to me afterward was overwhelming. Dougherty, Tom Smith, of the New Jersey State Police, Bob Bennett, from the New York police narcotics unit, and dozens of others came up and threw their arms around me, hugging me and shaking my hand. Quite a few tears were shed at that meeting. It was one of the greatest love experiences I have ever known.

As I mulled it over later, I was amazed at how the bitterness I had felt for these men, and all they represented, had now turned into unreserved love. The only thing the police and I once had in common was the desire to destroy one another. Only Christ made the difference.

Spencer Parker, the dyed-in-the-wool cop hater, now began to help organize and participate in policemen appreciation nights. I actually became the chaplain of the Northern New Jersey Fellowship of Christian Lawmen!

My wife and I spent time socializing with Deputy Chief Dougherty, Investigator Matt Rocco, and dozens of other law-enforcement officials. My life finally seemed to be moving ahead on the right track, on a predictable course that would leave me comfortable, happy, and secure for the rest of my days. But such was not to be the case. God's ways and timetables are not man's—I thought I had learned that lesson quite well. What I didn't realize was that God had plans to send me back once more to that difficult spiritual school of total trust and commitment to Him.

9

". . . Though I Was Blind, Now I See"

A man can plan his whole life and think he has every right to expect that his plans will come to pass if he prepares himself properly and works hard to achieve his goals. But sometimes freak accidents—or perhaps divine surprises—intervene to overturn every plan, no matter how perfectly conceived.

That's what happened to me one evening, as I was looking for some important papers in a closet in our home. Using a high-intensity lamp, I started probing around, trying to find what I was looking for on a high shelf, when the lamp touched a fluorescent lighting tube that had been stored in a corner. The fluorescent tube exploded right in my face. Except for some mild stinging, I didn't think anything was wrong at first, so I cleaned up the mess, washed my face, and went to bed.

The next morning, as I was driving Virginia and our two daughters downtown for a class they were attending, I noticed I had some trouble seeing clearly, but I didn't mention anything about it. To be safe, though, I stopped by a hospital on the way home and told the doctors what had happened to me.

They told me to drive immediately to the Newark Eye and Ear Hospital, and when I arrived there the specialists rushed me into an examination room and started checking me out. They told me I had some glass in my eyes, put a patch on my right eye, and told me to come back the next day. I still wasn't really too worried, but my vision did seem to be getting worse.

While attending a policemen's appreciation service

that night, where I was scheduled to give a talk, I found I had serious trouble finding the steps to the speaker's platform. Someone had to give me a hand. My friend, Deputy Chief Jack Dougherty, was also on the program, and he became worried as he watched me fumbling toward the lectern. On the way home that night, I had difficulty keeping the car on the road, but unbeknownst to me, a guardian angel was right behind me, keeping a sharp eye out for my well-being. Jack had decided to follow me in his own car, to be sure that I made it home safely.

I continued to go in for treatments, but my vision got worse and worse, until I could only see shadows. I had become legally blind, and the doctors still didn't know exactly what was wrong with me. They attached electrodes to my head and stimulated different parts of my brain in an effort to restore my sight. The treatments made me so sick I couldn't keep my food down, but it was all to no avail. I finally realized that I had to face squarely what had happened to me. I had become a blind man, and for all I knew, I would be blind for the rest of my life.

It was hard, at first, to see any purpose in God's allowing something like this to happen to me. *With all I had been through in my life, why not give me a little ease and happiness, Lord?* Some Christians didn't make my situation any easier, either.

"Spencer, you must be out of God's will, for something like this to happen to you!" one woman said. "You better look deep into your heart and find out what you've done wrong!"

"You're the only black person in the Pocket Testament League, and the Lord is doing this to you to chastise you for that!" someone else said.

It's a funny thing how people can seem to get messages from God for me, but not for themselves. Their comments didn't make any sense—especially when I realized that Job had faced the same sort of criticism, and yet he was still declared righteous by God. God allowed me to reflect deeply on Job during my first days of sightlessness, and I realized He had done a work in Job that brought glory and honor to His name. Perhaps the same thing was happening to me.

But it still wasn't easy for me to accept my condition, especially not when I got my first white cane and attempted to make it around the once-familiar streets of East Orange—streets that now presented themselves to me as an incomprehensible, shadowy, noisy maze. I learned that people don't know what to say to blind people—they either push past roughly and grumble at them, or they praise them too much.

After I had crossed one busy street by myself, one young man came up and said, "Hey, Dad, you're doing good with that white stick!"

He grabbed my cane, and I snapped, "Sir, let my stick go! I can't stand here in this traffic and talk to you."

"Tell me, Dad, how can you go across the street on the green light like that?"

"Sir," I replied gruffly, "if you don't mind, I have things to do!"

A counselor who had been assigned to advise me chuckled when I told him about the incident. "You're not going to change the world by getting mad at people," he said. "Just take it easy and be patient. They don't understand your situation."

Suddenly, I knew how right he was. I recalled how hostile I had been to blind people as a young man—how I had thought they were all phonies and how I had actually stolen money from them. It seemed that God had something to show me about this aspect of my past life, just as He had taught me some lessons about hating cops.

As I relived those days when I rejected and despised blind people who begged on street corners, I asked God's forgiveness. Then slowly He began to show me part of the plan He had for me as a blind person. I knew Jesus had told us to go into all the world and preach the Gospel, and after my blindness I did some research to see what the church had done to reach the blind.

I discovered that the blind are perhaps the most neglected group of all. Maybe we don't take the Gospel to the blind because we assume, consciously or subconsciously, that the sightless can't hear or think. I find that many people believe there's something wrong with my ability to reason, as well as with my eyesight—but that's just not the case. Since losing my sight, I've discovered that my memory has improved incredibly. I learned to appreciate my brain far more after the accident than I ever did before. People who can see tend to take things for granted, but the blind person has to think constantly.

I learned to write and read Braille, and soon I was teaching it at a school for the blind and using it as a vehicle to witness for Christ. I would write a question to one of my students: "It's nice to learn Braille, isn't it?"

"Yes."

"To whom shall we give thanks?" I'd write.

"The teacher."

"It's deeper than that. Don't you think God has something to do with the sensitivity of our fingers and with our brains?" I would reply through the raised symbols I produced on the Braille machine.

Through conversations like this, I tried to dispel the bitterness and frustration that blindness can bring, and substitute instead the confidence of a faith in Christ.

I've discovered, since I've been blind, that man is never without communication. Even if he can't hear or see, he can still communicate through touch and body contact. I've made myself understood to a man who couldn't see, hear, or talk, just by allowing him to put his fingers against my mouth as I talked. But even if we could feel nothing, God has made us so that we can still talk with Him through His Spirit. I've often told my students this, and concluded by saying, "We must praise God, even in our blindness."

It's amazing how my blindness has actually expanded my ministry, rather than limiting it. Now, I speak not only to law-enforcement groups, but also at many conferences for the handicapped. I still pray for the return of my sight, but I've learned to accept, as did the Apostle Paul, the weaknesses and imperfections of my body. And God seems to be saying to me, as He said to that apostle, "My grace is sufficient for you, for my power is made perfect in weakness" (2 Corinthians 12:9 RSV).

Blindness, I've learned, is not so much a problem of the body as of the spirit. Before I accepted Christ, I was in the same predicament that Paul described for all unbelievers: ". . . the god of this world has blinded the minds of the unbelievers, to keep them from seeing the light of the gospel of the glory of Christ, who is the likeness of God" (2 Corinthians 4:4 RSV). Physically, I was able to see perfectly, but all that I beheld was the shambles and lack of purpose of a life without God—a life steeped in crime, bitterness, and discontent. Now I could see clearly, and yet I was totally blind.

Even after I became a Christian, the darkness of sin sometimes passed over my eyes, as when I allowed the need for revenge to cloud my vision after I was wrongfully accused, convicted, and imprisoned for armed robbery. Even when I first lost my sight after the accident, I was tempted to let my physical problem become more important than my relationship with Christ. But He supported me and led me out of that spiritual darkness, into a new light of understanding in my relationship with Him. And even though my physical sight hasn't been restored, I can still say joyously, with that blind man Jesus healed in John 9:25: ". . . one thing I know, that though I was blind, now I see."

Afterword

I've written this book to give glory, honor, and praise to the Lord Jesus Christ, who preserved my mind during the five-month ordeal in the hospital for the criminally insane. As you have read, I believe I was injected with a chemical that was designed to destroy certain brain tissues and establish control over my aggressive criminal behavior. Some men have died from this form of treatment, and others have been reduced to subhuman beings, with no ability to think or reason for themselves. I escaped that fate—but not through my own power.

After I had finished my last prison term, I was attending a church service where the congregation was singing the hymn "The Love of God." I noticed an asterisk and looked down to the bottom of the page. An explanatory note said the last stanza of the song was found scribbled on the wall of the narrow room of an insane asylum, where a supposedly deranged man was staying. I immediately knew God had not deserted that man, just as He didn't desert me.

I pray and trust the Lord that as you have read this book and seen how the Lord brought me out of that horrible pit of insanity, you will feel a burden for the countless numbers who are still in mental institutions, without any hope. Many of these lost souls will never see a free society again, and will never know what it means to be saved by the power and blood of the Lord Jesus Christ.

I also hope that you will hear the lost souls in these mental hospitals as they cry, "Is it nothing to you, all ye [Christians] that pass by? behold and see if there be any sorrow like unto my sorrow, which is done unto me . . ." (Lamentations 1:12). This is the most desperate cry that could ever be uttered by any human being. I was there, and I know the depths of such a cry.

I know the tears, hurts, and longings of the human soul, the pain of minds deadened with drugs. I know the cries of those whom I have left behind, who moan, "No man cared for my soul." I am sure that no one can ever understand such a cry as well as the Christians who have the burden, compassion, and vision for souls and who see through eyes opened by the Lord Himself.

I praise God that I can feel the meaning of these cries, for I know that tomorrow may be too late to listen if we fail to reach these perishing souls *now*— today—with the Gospel of Christ.